MAR 2 6 2013

iMath
Readers

A Day at Mini-Golf:
What's the Length?

by Donna Loughran

Content Consultant
David T. Hughes
Mathematics Curriculum Specialist

NORWOOD HOUSE PRESS
Chicago, IL

Norwood House Press
PO Box 316598
Chicago, IL 60631

For information regarding Norwood House Press, please visit our website at
www.norwoodhousepress.com or call 866-565-2900.

Special thanks to: Heidi Doyle
Production Management: Six Red Marbles
Editors: Linda Bullock and Kendra Muntz
Printed in Heshan City, Guangdong, China. 208N—012013

Library of Congress Cataloging-in-Publication Data

Loughran, Donna.

    A day at mini-golf: what's the length? / by Donna Loughran; consultant,
David T. Hughes.
    p. cm.—(iMath)

    Includes bibliographical references and index.
    Summary: "The mathematical concept of units of measurement is introduced
as a family plays mini-golf. Readers learn how to measure the length of an object
in standard and metric units, using inches, feet, yards, centimeters, and meters.
Additional concepts include estimating lengths, length units, and measurement
tools. This book features a discover activity, history connection, and
mathematical vocabulary introduction"—Provided by publisher.
    Audience: Ages 6–8
    Audience: K to grade 3
    ISBN: 978-1-59953-556-2 (library edition: alk. paper)
    ISBN: 978-1-60357-525-6 (ebook)

    1. Length measurement—Juvenile literature.
    2. Standards of length—Juvenile literature.
    3. Golf courses—Juvenile literature.
    4. Miniature golf—Juvenile literature. I. Title.

    QC102.L678 2012
    530.8—dc23
    2012035749

CONTENTS

Note to Caregivers:

Throughout this book, many questions are posed to the reader. Some are open-ended and ask what the reader thinks. Discuss these questions with your child and guide him or her in thinking through the possible answers and outcomes. There are also questions posed which have a specific answer. Encourage your child to read through the text to determine the correct answer. Most importantly, encourage answers grounded in reality while also allowing imaginations to soar. Information to help support you as you share the book with your child is provided in the back in the **Additional Notes** section.

Bold words are defined in the glossary in the back of the book.

Welcome to Mini-Golf!

You are going mini-golfing! Choose a colorful ball. Take a club. Practice your swing. You will think about length along the way.

The rules of mini-golf are easy. There are eighteen green lanes, called holes. To begin, place your ball on the tee area. That's the start of a hole. Look for the cup at the other end of the lane. That's where the ball should go.

Estimate the **distance** to the hole. That is, guess about how far away the hole is. How many swings will it take to reach the cup? Each swing is a point. The person with the fewest points at the end of the game wins!

Get ready to measure. A mini-golf adventure is coming your way!

Different Ways to Measure

When you **measure** length, you find out how long something is. You can measure length in many different ways. You can use an object to measure. You can compare objects. Or you can use a measurement tool.

Idea 1: Use **an object** to measure. For example, you can use paper clips. Put them end to end to measure length.

How long is the pencil? Is using an object a good way to measure?

Sometimes, you can compare lengths. Look at the picture. Which pencil is the longest? Which is the shortest?

Idea 2: Use standard unit measuring tools, such as a **ruler**, a **yardstick**, or a **tape measure**. These are often marked in **inches**, **feet**, and **yards**.

A ruler is 12 inches long. A yardstick is three feet long, or 36 inches long. A tape measure is much longer. It is marked in inches, feet, and yards.

How long is the pencil? Is using a ruler a good way to measure?

Idea 3: Use metric unit measuring tools, such as a **metric ruler**, a **meter stick**, or a **meter tape**. These are often marked in **centimeters** and **meters**.

How long is the pencil? Is using a metric ruler a good way to measure?

What metric measuring tool might you use to measure the length of a brick? What about the length of a brick wall?

Discover Activity

Measure Up

Materials
- ruler
- yardstick
- tape measure in inches, feet, and yards
- pencil
- paper

With a friend or family member, take turns naming objects in the room.

Estimate, or guess, about how long the objects are. Use inches first. Then, use feet.

Write your guesses on a piece of paper. Keep them a secret!

Tape measure

Then, use a ruler, a yardstick, or a measuring tape to measure the length of the object. Write the measurement next to your guess. The person whose guess is closest to the exact length wins one point.

Keep playing. The first person to earn 10 points wins the game!

Let's Play!

Molly and Polly are twins. Today they are going with their cousin, Ben, to play mini-golf.

"We are going to a mini-golf park. You're going to enjoy it!" Ben says.

At the park, Polly points to a pirate. "Look!" she says. "This is a pirate park."

Ben grins. "You will see more than pirates here," he says.

Ben's parents buy tickets. They give the children their golf clubs and golf balls.

"This is the first hole," Ben says. "We must hit the ball under the castle. The cup is on the other side."

Molly puts her ball on the ground at the tee area. She swings her golf club. The ball bounces off the castle wall. She tries again. This time, the ball rolls under the castle.

"Where did it go?" Molly asks.

"Look on the other side," Ben says. They walk behind the castle. There is Molly's ball. Molly walks to her ball. She swings her club again. The ball rolls into the cup.

"I did it!" Molly says proudly.

"Look!" Ben says. He points to a whale at the next hole. Polly touches the whale's teeth. "They are sharp!" she says.

They take turns. Ben's ball rolls around inside the whale's mouth. Then, it rolls out again. Molly's ball does the same. Finally, Polly swings. Her ball barely moves.

"I wonder how far each ball is from the cup," Polly says. She starts at the whale. Then, she walks heel-to-toe along the lane.

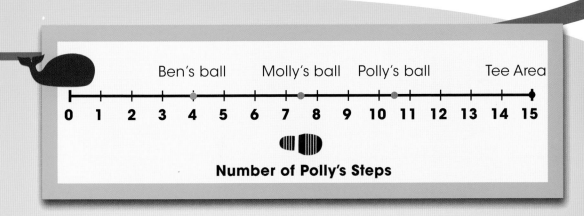

Who is closest to the hole? How do you know?

How far is Ben's ball from Molly's?

Who has to make the longest shot to make the hole?

"Ooh, lizards!" Molly says at the next hole. She bends down to pet the giant green head.

"I don't see the cup," Polly says.

Molly peeks under the lizard. "There it is," she says. "But where does the ball come out again?"

"I bet it comes out at the next hole," Ben says. "There's only one way to find out."

Ben swings. The ball disappears under the lizard. The children hear a rattle as the ball rolls through a tunnel. It pops out of a wall at the next hole.

"You're right!" Molly says.

Polly and Molly take turns. Their balls roll under the lizard and disappear. At the next hole, they face a giant shoe. "I would like to meet the person who wears that shoe!" laughs Polly.

One by one, the children hit their balls. Each ball stops before the hole.

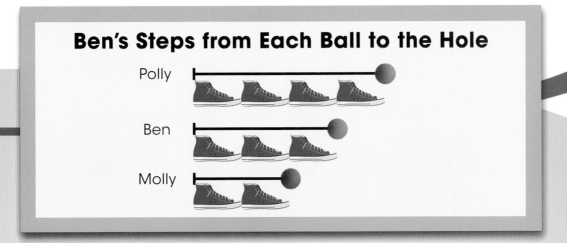

Ben's Steps from Each Ball to the Hole

Polly

Ben

Molly

Who is closest to the hole?

How many steps does Ben take from Polly's ball to the hole?

How many steps closer is Molly than Polly to the hole?

Math at Work

How does someone plan a mini-golf course? First, a designer looks at the empty land. It could be flat. It could be hilly. There could be water, like a pond or river. Where could the holes go? She looks and measures the land carefully. Next, the designer thinks of a theme. A theme is a subject, like pirates.

Then, the designer draws a plan. She plans for both easy and difficult holes. She adds objects, like giant animals. These make the course more fun to play. She may add ponds and bridges. She gives her plans to builders and artists.

Builders follow the designer's plans. They use the designer's measurements. Artists make the animal figures. At last, everything is ready. It's just as the designer imagined!

A designer drew a plan for this mini-golf course along a beach.

Astronaut Alan Shepard was the first American in space. He was also the first astronaut to play golf on the Moon.

Connecting to History

Alan Shepard was an **astronaut**. In 1961, he became the first American to go into space. He flew 116 miles above Earth. His flight lasted almost 16 minutes.

In 1971, Shepard was the team leader of *Apollo 14*. He and another astronaut made two moonwalks. They collected lots of moon rocks. They also had fun playing golf!

While standing on the Moon, Shepard hit three golf balls. These golf balls are still on the Moon today.

Join the Clubs!

"Look," says Ben. "That horse is wearing cowboy boots!"

Molly adds, "I like the **armadillo** riding the horse." She points to the gray animal on top.

"How far do you think it is from here to the armadillo?" asks Polly.

Molly says, "I know how we can find out."

"Let's use our clubs to measure. Let's lay them on the ground so they touch. But, they can't **overlap**. Then, we will count them."

How many golf clubs is it to the armadillo?

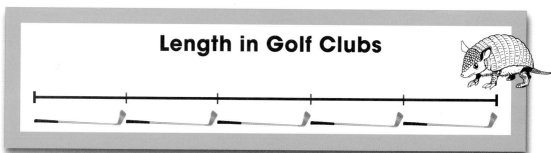

Length in Golf Clubs

"This is going to be a hard hole," Polly says. "Look at the space between the dice. It isn't very wide."

Polly swings her golf club. Her ball curves to the left. It hits the corner of one number block, and it rolls away. She picks up the ball.

"Try again, Polly," says Molly. "You can do it."

This time, the ball rolls between the blocks. It slows down. Suddenly, it plops into the cup. "Yeah!" the girls yell.

How far apart are the blocks?

 What's the Word?

Have you ever wanted to play golf? Read the *ABC's of Golf* by Susan Greene. Learn more about golf and the items you need to play the game.

Ben's Favorite Hole

"This is my favorite hole," Ben says. "I love dinosaurs. This one is a T-rex!"

"It's great!" Molly says, looking up at the giant teeth.

"The dinosaur is so colorful!" says Polly. "But where's the cup?"

"It's by the dinosaur's tail," says Ben. "I don't know how far away that is, though. How can we find out?"

The mini-golf course owner walks past the group. "I can help you measure," he says. A ruler, an old yardstick, and a meter tape are inside his toolbox.

Molly asks, "How will we measure?"

Idea 1: Use **an object**. "We can use our feet to measure," says Polly. "But my feet are shorter than yours, Ben. So, our measures would be different."

Idea 2: Use a **ruler**, a **yardstick**, or a **tape measure** to measure in **inches**, **feet**, or **yards**.

Ben says, "A ruler works better for short lengths. This old yardstick would make it easier to measure how far away the hole is."

Idea 3: Use a **metric ruler**, a **meter stick**, or a **meter tape** to measure in **centimeters** or **meters**. Polly says, "This meter tape is new. Let's use it to measure."

Ben says, "You go first, Polly. I'm sure you can make it to the cup in two swings. We can measure how far the ball travels with each swing."

Ben is right. Polly's ball goes in the hole after two swings. Polly swings twice. She measures, "1 meter, 2 meters, 3 meters…" How far did Polly's ball travel to the cup?

Molly plays next. She swings once. Then, she swings again. On the third swing, the ball rolls around the cup. Then, plop! It goes in. "I'm getting better!" Molly says. "I'm glad there are more holes to play!"

Ben grins and says, "Yes, lots more. Wait until you see what's hiding behind the dinosaur!"

What Comes Next?

Design your own mini-golf course!
Follow these steps:

1. Measure a space for your mini-golf course.

2. Choose a theme for your course. Will you have sea and land animals? Will you have make-believe animals? Will you use fairy tale characters?

3. Design a mix of both easy and hard holes.

4. Draw a picture of your mini-golf course the way a bird would see it from the sky. Share your picture with your family and friends.

GLOSSARY

armadillo: an animal with bony plates and bands over its body. Armadillos live in North, Central, and South America.

astronaut: a person who goes into space.

centimeter(s): a small measure on a meter scale, about the width of a fingertip.

distance: the length between two objects or places.

estimate: to figure out about how much. To use a number that is close to a real amount.

feet: 12 inches equal one foot. Three feet equal one yard.

inch(es): a small measure, about as long as from your fingertip to your first knuckle.

measure: to use an object or tool to find out how long something is.

meter(s): a measure on a meter stick, about as far as the distance from the floor to a door knob.

meter stick: a ruler that is 100 centimeters long.

meter tape: a very long ruler that unrolls to measure length. It is marked in centimeters and meters.

metric ruler: a piece of wood or plastic marked in centimeters.

object: a thing, such as a golf club or golf ball.

overlap: to cross over.

ruler: a piece of wood or plastic marked in inches.

tape measure: a very long ruler that unrolls to measure length. It is marked in inches, feet, and yards.

yard(s): a measure of three feet, about as long as from your nose to the tip of your fingers.

yardstick: a ruler that is three feet long.

FURTHER READING

FICTION

Measuring Penny, by Loreen Leedy, Henry Holt and Co., 1998

SpongeBob Tees Off, by Ilanit Oliver, Simon Spotlight, 2012

NONFICTION

How Do You Measure Length and Distance? by Thomas K. and Heather Adamson, Capstone Press, 2011

Measurement, by Penny Dowdy, Crabtree Publishing Company, 2008

Additional Notes

The page references below provide answers to questions asked throughout the book. Questions whose answers will vary are not addressed.

Page 6: The pencil is 3 paper clips long. The purple pencil is longest. The orange pencil is shortest.

Page 7: The pencil is 4 inches long. The pencil is 10 centimeters long. You might use a metric ruler to measure a brick. You would use a meter tape to measure a brick wall.

Page 11: Ben is closest to the hole. Ben's ball is between 3 and 4 steps away from Molly's ball. Polly has to make the longest shot to the hole.

Page 13: Molly is closest to the hole. It is 4 of Ben's steps from Polly's ball to the hole. Molly is 2 steps closer to the hole than Polly is.

Page 16: It is 5 golf clubs to the armadillo.

Page 17: The blocks are 10 inches apart.

Page 20: The ball travels 8 meters to the cup.

INDEX

Content Consultant

David T. Hughes

David is an experienced mathematics teacher, writer, presenter, and adviser. He serves as a consultant for the Partnership for Assessment of Readiness for College and Careers. David has also worked as the Senior Program Coordinator for the Charles A. Dana Center at The University of Texas at Austin and was an editor and contributor for the *Mathematics Standards in the Classroom* series.